TEEN MENTAL HEALTH™

self-esteem

Betsy S. Morrison
and Ruth Ann Ruiz

ROSEN
PUBLISHING®

New York

Published in 2012 by The Rosen Publishing Group, Inc.
29 East 21st Street, New York, NY 10010

First Edition

Library of Congress Cataloging-in-Publication Data

Morrison, Betsy S.
Self-esteem / Betsy S. Morrison, Ruth Ann Ruiz.—1st ed.
    p. cm.—(Teen mental health)
Includes bibliographical references and index.
ISBN 978-1-4488-4587-3 (library binding)
1. Self-esteem. 2. Adolescent psychology. I. Ruiz, Ruth Ann. II. Title.
BF697.5.S46M665 2011
155.5'18—dc22

2011008646

Manufactured in the United States of America

CPSIA Compliance Information: Batch #S11YA: For further information, contact Rosen Publishing, New York, New York, at 1-800-237-9932.

contents

chapter one   Your Self-Worth   **4**

chapter two   Building Your Confidence   **13**

chapter three   Confidence and Success   **22**

chapter four   Setting Goals   **28**

chapter five   The Aim for Excellence   **35**

glossary   **43**

for more information   **44**

for further reading   **46**

index   **47**

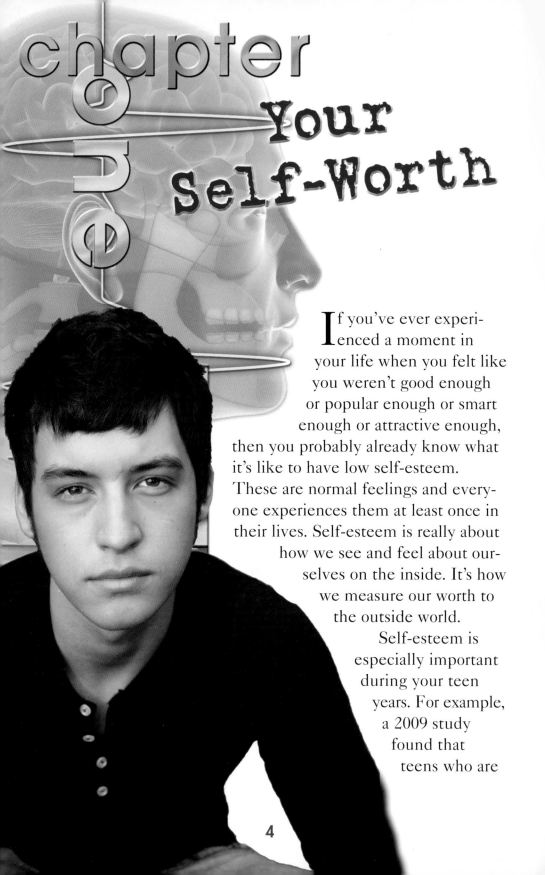

chapter one

Your Self-Worth

I f you've ever experi-
enced a moment in
your life when you felt like
you weren't good enough
or popular enough or smart
enough or attractive enough,
then you probably already know what
it's like to have low self-esteem.
These are normal feelings and everyone experiences them at least once in
their lives. Self-esteem is really about
how we see and feel about ourselves on the inside. It's how
we measure our worth to
the outside world.
Self-esteem is
especially important
during your teen
years. For example,
a 2009 study
found that
teens who are

4

Low self-esteem is sometimes tied to a poor body image. Many teens find flaws in themselves that sometimes aren't really there. The pressure for perfection in society is very strong.

overweight, or believed themselves to be, are more likely to attempt suicide than other teens. Researchers believe the problem stems from the low self-esteem that can result from the pressure to fit into an unrealistic standard of beauty. Regular depression screenings and obesity prevention programs are positive steps. But clearly the dangers of low self-esteem are real for many teens.

Confidence

Do you ever feel like you can't do anything right? Have you ever felt like you have nothing to offer the world? If you did, you're not the only one who's had little or no confidence in themselves. So don't worry. All of us doubt our abilities at some time or another. It's how each of us deals with those feelings, which separate those who go after what they want and those who are too afraid to try at all. If you let those feelings of doubt and insecurity completely take over your life, then you may never reach your full potential. The good news is that you're in charge of your self-confidence. Just because it's low now, doesn't mean it has to stay that way. You can start building up your self-confidence right now by discovering what your real talents are and what truly makes you happy. When other people see that you feel good about yourself, you will have changed how the world sees you, too.

Your Mirror of Self-Reflection

The best way to figure out your level of self-esteem and confidence is to take a close look at yourself. When you get dressed in the morning, you like to check yourself out in the mirror to make sure you look good, right? Well this is the same thing, except you're going to use a different kind of mirror. This mirror isn't made of glass. This mirror is in your head. We'll call it the mirror of self-reflection. Examine who you are and how you feel about yourself and your life. Very few people do this, because they fear that they might not like what they see. But to build your self-confidence, you have to start with the reality of who you are and how you feel about yourself. As you begin to look at yourself, consider these questions:

- Do you like who you are?
- Do you believe in yourself?
- Do you think you can do the things that you want to do?
- Do you like the things that happen in your life?
- Do you feel that you have any control over your life and how others see you?
- Do you think that you are as talented and valued as other people?

If you answered no to most or all of these questions, you probably lack self-confidence and have low self-esteem. If this is the case, you are definitely not alone. Most people have some form of low self-confidence, no matter how sure of themselves they may seem. In a 1999 interview with the Dutch magazine *Avant Garde* actor Johnny Depp admitted to having very little confidence in himself when he was in high school. "As a teenager I was so insecure. I was the type of guy that never fit in because

In a 1999 interview, actor Johnny Depp admitted to having low self-esteem when he was younger. Today, Depp is an Oscar-nominated actor who is widely regarded as one of the greatest of his generation.

he never dared to choose. I was convinced I had absolutely no talent at all. For nothing. And that thought took away all my ambition, too." In fact, it wasn't until Depp realized that he had a talent for playing music that his opinion of himself began to change. Eventually, he also discovered a talent for acting.

What Is Your Comfort Zone?

Losing confidence in yourself is a normal part of life. Having confidence and not having it often goes in a cycle, almost like the way seasons change from one to another. So, don't be alarmed if you don't feel as good about your self anymore. It happens to all of us. In fact, it actually serves a purpose in protecting you from more bad experiences. Poor self-confidence and low self-esteem provides a risk-free "comfort zone" where you can hide. You won't feel "comfortable" in this comfort zone, but at least you won't risk anything by staying there. This "comfort" seems easier than working to improve yourself. But something strange happens in the comfort zone—you end up using more energy staying where you are than you would use by developing your talents.

Alone in the Zone

Suppose you move to a new state. Perhaps you were really good at a sport such as swimming, but you are nervous about trying out for the new school's swim team. As you wait to dive into the pool, your hands get very cold and your legs start shaking. You have never felt this way about swimming before. You think to yourself, "If I don't do

Making friends can be challenging, especially if you are naturally quiet and shy. But it is important to remember that your number of friends does not determine your self-worth.

well now, I won't make the team and the others will think I'm a loser." You walk around nervously but you can't shake the chill. When your turn comes, you might dive into the pool and swim well. But, because you are so anxious, you are likely to perform poorly. You may even decide to give up and not try out at all.

Your lack of self-confidence may also lead to difficulty in making friends. You may be so afraid of what your classmates think of you that you choose not to introduce yourself at all. You might say to yourself, "I'm no better off, but I'm no worse off either. Better safe than sorry." You don't feel good about making new friends, but at least you won't lose any. However, if you don't let people get to know you, then they can only form an opinion based on your shyness or unfriendly behavior.

After a while, the false safety of the comfort zone starts to run your life. Eventually it can ruin your life by keeping you from growing as a person and meeting new people who could help change your life. The loneliness can also lead to feelings of depression.

Breaking Out of the Comfort Zone

You have to be willing to break out of this comfort zone to get the things you want in life. If you never ask someone out on a date, you won't be rejected, but you'll never experience any romance. Don't be afraid of rejection or failure. They're a part of life and often a launchpad to personal growth. It's very important, though, that you never see yourself as a reject or a failure. You're a human being like everyone else. You have strengths and weaknesses like everyone else. Find your strengths and you will begin to see yourself in a whole new light. Then, everyone else will see the new you, too.

10 Great Questions to Ask Your Guidance Counselor or Therapist

1. Do I have low self-esteem because I'm depressed?

2. Am I destined to be a failure in life because I've never been good at anything?

3. How can I recognize my strengths and weaknesses?

4. Is my self-esteem related to my physical appearance?

5. Should I try to make new friends by doing everything exactly the way they do?

6. Will I need to change everything about myself to have more confidence?

7. How will self-confidence help me with meeting new people?

8. What are some techniques I can use to feel better about myself?

9. How can my family and friends help me raise my self-esteem and confidence?

10. What should I do if my low self-esteem keeps getting worse and worse?

chapter TWO
Building Your Confidence

Our lives are often guided by caution. Some caution is good since it prevents us from walking into oncoming traffic or eating spoiled food. But when caution controls you too much, you stop growing. People with low self-esteem often build walls around themselves to protect them from getting their feelings hurt or looking foolish. While these walls won't let anyone in to make you feel worse about yourself, they don't let you out to experience good things, either.

Having positive self-esteem can help you perform well during a job interview. Even if you aren't feeling your most confident beforehand, it may help to give yourself a pep talk.

Push back your protective mental walls to be more of who you can be. The walls are there to protect you from harm, but unless you expand the space within the walls, you stop living and become like a programmed robot.

If you keep telling yourself that nobody wants to be your friend, then you won't let anyone become your friend. By believing the negative things that you think about yourself, you are setting yourself up for disappointment. If you believe that nobody will ever hire you, then you're not going to bother looking for a job. Or, you might go on a job interview, but you'll convince yourself that they won't like you. What you think is what you get. Good things are out there waiting for you, but not if you've convinced yourself that there are only bad things.

The Effects of Self-Talk on Confidence

Poor self-confidence is manufactured. It is not your fate, even though you may think it is.

People manufacture self-confidence by using self-talk. Self-talk is simply what you tell yourself. You talk to yourself all the time, in the form of either words or feelings. At times you may feel happy, whereas at other times you may feel down or depressed. You may think, "This is cool" or "This sucks." You might say to yourself, "That was nice" or "That was really bad." All of these reactions are self-talk.

The kinds of things you say to yourself all day are very important. They help create your attitudes, your expectations, and your actions. The things that you say to yourself over and over sink deep into your mind. They become a big part of your idea network.

Self-talk is like a powerful drug. It can be a harmful narcotic that destroys you and your life, or it can be penicillin that heals you and helps make you stronger.

The Cycle of Negative Self-Talk

You manufacture low self-confidence and low self-esteem when you get caught in the cycle of negative self-talk. This cycle has nothing to do with things, people, or events outside of you. It has everything to do with the way you think about those things, people, or events.

There are several types of negative self-talk that create low self-esteem. They can occur separately on their own or all together at the same time.

The Push to Be Perfect

If you think you have to be perfect to be acceptable, you'll never be acceptable because you'll never be per-

Nobody is perfect. Don't let your grades in school affect your self-worth. If you get a disappointing grade, see a teacher for extra help or study harder for the next quiz.

fect. There's nothing wrong with getting a "B" on a test, but if you're always expecting to get "A's," then you're just setting yourself up for a big disappointment when there is no need to feel that way.

If you were really perfect, life would be very boring. There would be nothing for you to learn or create. Be glad you aren't perfect. No person on earth is perfect. We can choose to grow and learn from good and bad experiences, not just the good ones.

Negative Judgments

We make negative judgments about ourselves and other people. We set such high standards that nobody can measure up to them, including ourselves. Judgmental thinking can keep us from appreciating anyone's best efforts at something, especially our own.

Negative judgments about yourself and others alienate you from those who might help or befriend you. As a result, we feel lonely, and loneliness makes low self-esteem worse.

External Control

In psychology this kind of thinking is called external control. We see ourselves as being controlled by parents, teachers, friends, society, and life. We feel helpless and see our situation as hopeless. Sometimes, a student might decide to drop out of school because they think the teachers don't like him or her, anyway, so there's no point in sticking around.

This thinking often takes the form of "I wish I could, but…" By indulging in it, you lock yourself into a prison of your own making. "I wish I could ask that person out on a date, but I have braces, so they're not going to want to go out with me if I have braces." These thoughts also become a form of judgmental thinking that only adds to the loneliness.

Avoiding Impoverished Thinking

We tell ourselves that we would feel better if we just had something that is missing in our lives such as more money or new clothes or the coolest cell phone. When you think

Mary J. Blige is known as the Queen of Hip-Hop Soul. But she wasn't always on top of the world. Even after she found success in music, she was still unhappy and insecure at times.

like this, it allows you to accept your misery since you don't have the things that you think you need to feel better about yourself. "If only" thinking doesn't work. Basing your ideas of yourself on what you own can't make you confident. Confidence must come from within. People who have all the money in the world can still feel insecure and worthless.

Mary J. Blige, who is often called the Queen of Hip-Hop Soul, didn't always feel like a queen, even after the success of her early albums. Blige struggled with drug and alcohol abuse, unhealthy relationships, and low self-esteem. As she worked through her problems, though, she eventually found the strength inside of her to overcome them. In a 2005 interview with MP3.com, Blige explained how fame and fortune were not enough to heal her emotional scars. "Like, it's real stuff that I have to deal with. So I'm not putting money in front of my insecurity, I'm dealing with my insecurity. There was a time when I used to pile a bunch of jewelry and clothes and furs on top of my insecurity, and then that's all I was, was jewelry and clothes and furs."

Seeing Ourselves as Victims

When we don't face reality and don't take responsibility for our reality, we tend to see ourselves as victims. Victim thinking causes us to see reality as beyond our control. We feel we cannot take any responsibility for what happens to us. Pushed to the extreme, this kind of thinking causes us to hate ourselves because we seem so weak. You might say to say yourself, "It's not my fault that I don't have any friends, everybody at this school already knows each other, they don't even know that I'm alive."

19

The Low Self-Esteem Trap

The first step in changing yourself is to be aware of these erroneous beliefs. You have to know what the problem is before you can do anything about it. Becoming aware of what you are doing to yourself is the first step. You can build your new confidence by avoiding the negative self-talk trap. We all want to avoid making mistakes. To do so, our instinct is to be cautious and follow the rules rather than being creative. Sometimes, we inflict these rules on ourselves so we don't risk failure or rejection.

Remember when you were learning to ride a bike? You probably fell down many times. But you kept getting up and trying it again even though some times you were bruised or scratched from the fall. Finally you were able to ride without help or falling down. Riding a bike was scary at first, but you let go of your fears. At some point you have to let go of your fears and take some risks.

You Have the Power of Choice

People who have lost confidence in themselves usually believe in luck. Relying on luck to solve your problems relieves you of any sense of responsibility. But as soon as you choose to take responsibility for what happens in your life, you begin to see that things you used to attribute to luck actually are the result of choices you make.

Make the decision now to change your life by changing the way you think about yourself. This moment of decision gives you the power of choice—it's your choice to improve your self-esteem.

MYTHS AND FACTS

Myth: Good self-esteem is a trait you either have or you don't have.

Fact: Good self-esteem is something that can be achieved through positive thinking and finding happiness by accepting yourself. It is a choice. It's not like being able to sing: it's something that anyone is capable of with the right attitude.

Myth: In order to improve my self-esteem and confidence, I must see a therapist.

Fact: You can improve your self-esteem and confidence on your own with the help of books and online tools that are available in your school library or in your guidance counselor's office. Family and friends can also be very helpful.

Myth: Self-confident people are always happy.

Fact: Even though they seem to be happy most of the time, self-confident people do experience painful emotions. They doubt themselves and their abilities, too, sometimes. It's a normal part of life to occasionally lose your confidence.

Myth: Once I improve my self-esteem, I will always be confident.

Fact: You may find that you will spend less time thinking about your confidence after you work on it. But you will have times throughout your life when your confidence will drop and you will need to work on it again.

chapter three

Confidence and Success

If you see yourself as a meaningless person leading a purposeless life, you will not be able to manufacture self-confidence and self-esteem. You will need to begin to see your life as having value in our world. Successful people believe that they have something to contribute to society just by being themselves. Your confidence will increase as you grow to believe that your life has value. Repairing your self-esteem and self-confidence is not going to be an easy task. You're going to need to be patient with yourself. With time and effort, you will get to know the new you like you would get to know another person.

You Can Find Meaning in Your Life

Dr. Viktor Frankl was imprisoned in a Nazi concentration camp during World War II. In his book about his experiences *Man's Search for Meaning*, he writes that the prisoners who gave up on themselves and lost their will to live also lost any sense of meaning in their lives. They were not able to go on, and they died.

Writing yourself notes can help build your positive self-talk. Think of things that you like about yourself or things you're good at and write them down.

23

The prisoners who did not lose the will to live kept focused on the idea that their lives had purpose. No matter how sick and frail they became, they were alive when the Allied armies liberated the camps. If they could do this in a brutal concentration camp where they faced death every moment of every day, you can do the same no matter what you have to face in your daily life.

Many people do not like what they see when they look at themselves. Try thinking of yourself this way: "There is only one me in all of human history. I am here for a reason. I have a talent that the world needs. If I don't develop my talent, the world will never have it. I need to become everything I was meant to be. I am here for a reason." Even better, write it down. Make little notes for yourself and stick them where you'll see them.

A self-confident person who has good self-esteem will always try to overcome any problem and accomplish whatever he or she needs in life. It doesn't mean they will always succeed, but it won't stop them from trying again. On the other hand, someone who has no self-confidence, no self-esteem, and no sense of meaning in his or her life will usually give up at the first sign of trouble. Which kind of person will you choose to be?

New Self-Talk

The kinds of things you say to yourself all day are very important. They help create your attitudes, your expectations, and your actions. The things that you say to yourself over and over sink deep into your mind. They become a big part of your idea network. Replace the old, negative self-talk with new, positive self-talk that will build your self-confidence. With positive self-talk, it's important to remember that you should never use words like "but" or "maybe." These are the kinds of words that will only hold you back.

Positive self-talk has four qualities:

- **It's personal:** Since your negative thoughts are about you, you must talk directly to yourself with your new self-talk. Use "I" in your new belief statements.
- **It's in the present tense:** Use self-talk about today, not about the past or the future. The past exists only as lessons you can remember. The future, by definition, never arrives. Speak about your new goals as if they were here with you now. Use present-tense verbs.
- **Positive attributes:** You get what you focus on, so focus on what you want, not on what you don't want. There's no point in dwelling on the worst-case scenario. You need to visualize the best possible outcome.
- **Power:** Do you tell yourself, "I'm an idiot! I'll never succeed! I'm a failure!"? These are strong statements. Make your new self-talk equally powerful in a positive way, showing how much fun you are having aiming at your new goals.

Using Thought Reversal

Your mind cannot believe two opposite thoughts at the same time. You can short-circuit negative thoughts by replacing them with positive ones. In psychology, this is called "thought reversal."

Think of the worst horror movie you've ever seen. Think of how grim and scary it was. Remember every detail that you can and really concentrate on them. Notice what is happening to your thoughts and feelings as you do this.

Now erase that idea. Think of a beautiful spring day in a meadow. See the warm light of the sun on the green grass. Look at the bright colors of all the new flowers. Smell the fresh air and listen to the birds. Notice what is happening to your thoughts and feelings now.

The horror movie scene and the pleasant spring meadow exist only in your mind, but both create powerful feelings and emotions. Wherever your thoughts and emotions go, your energy goes. You can create negative energy or positive energy. It all depends on what thoughts you choose.

Self-Doubt

In the past you've invested lots of time in making your negative self-talk come true. Don't be surprised now when the old thoughts pop up. Be ready when your mind raises doubts.

Doubts are normal. But be ready to counteract them so that you don't become overcautious. Tell yourself, "That's the reality. So what? Now what?"

Let's see why this three-part statement is a powerful cure for doubts:

"That's the reality." Most people lose confidence because they are afraid that something might go wrong. It's up to you to choose to learn and grow from the mistake or to let the mistake keep you from trying again.

"So what?" This question takes away the heavy mental burden that keeps many people worried. You accept that things may not go the way you planned. Mistakes are stepping-stones toward success.

"Now what?" This question refocuses you on the present moment. You can choose new behavior right now. Every new moment gives you the opportunity to make new choices.

Seeing Success in Yourself

When you talk to yourself in a positive way, you support yourself and make yourself strong. You feel better about yourself. You gain a better self-image, a more positive image of who you really are. With a good self-image, you are more likely to have good things happen in your life.

In the same way, you can gain a better image of yourself by choosing to see yourself in a better light. By imagining or picturing yourself in a more positive way, you become more positive.

chapter four

Setting Goals

As you begin to work on improving your self-confidence and self-esteem you will need to start by setting your sights on a destination that you would like to reach and a guide to get you there. If you don't know where you are going, you'll end up someplace else. If you start off on a trip and you have no clue what the destination is, how will you know if you have ever reached your destination? What if you start a trip and you don't know how to get there?

There is an old saying, "No wind favors a

ship without a destination." Imagine a ship in the middle of the ocean. If the ship has nowhere to go, the crew can't set the sails to make use of any wind. The ship just drifts. People who have no goals in life just drift.

But if the captain of the ship has a destination, he can have the crew set the sails to make use of any wind, even a wind blowing in the opposite direction. Unfortunately, many people have little idea of what they can achieve in life, and thus they aim at nothing. They feel frustrated, and their self-esteem remains low.

What Is a Good Goal?

If you think it is farfetched to plan ahead five years, remember, "No wind favors a ship without a destination." If you don't consider where you want to be in five years, you could just drift for five years and end up wherever the winds of life blow you. Then you will feel frustrated. That is no way to build confidence.

Ask yourself:

- Do I have any goals?
- How specific are they?
- What do I want to be doing a year from now?
- What do I need to do to reach my goal a year from now?
- What do I want to be doing five years from now?

Look at the successful people in life. They have something most other people don't have. It's not money, cars, possessions, or big houses, although they may have all those things. They got where they are because they had goals, and they kept their goals in sight all the time. They manufactured their self-esteem by knowing where they wanted to go, and then they did what it took to get there. Talk to some of the people in your own life whom you consider successful. Maybe, they can point you in the right direction.

Breaking Your Goals Down

When choosing your goals, it's important not to do too much all at once. Sometimes, we get so caught up in the

If your goal is to talk to someone you are romantically interested in, start slowly by just saying hi in the hallway at school.

goal itself, that we feel completely overwhelmed by it. In order to avoid feeling overwhelmed, you should break your big goal down into smaller, more manageable goals. If your goal feels like it'll take too long or if it seems too unrealistic, then focus on the smaller goals that will achieve the larger goal.

Changing "I Can't" to "I Can"

A confident person does not believe in "can't." Suppose President John F. Kennedy had allowed "can't" to control the space program. In 1960, when he announced his goal to have an American on the moon within ten years, manned space flight was considered pure science fiction. The scientific community said it was impossible.

"Why is it impossible?" he asked. "Because we don't have the metal, the fuel, and the technology," they responded. He told them to get the metal, the fuel, and the technology. "Can't" was changed to "can" and on July 20, 1969, the first man set foot on the moon.

Taking It Step by Step

When you find out the specific reasons why you "can't," you have actually identified the ways you "can." You know the steps that make it possible to do what you thought was impossible. Instead of viewing a seemingly impossible goal as one huge job, you break the job down into its smaller parts and then do each part step-by-step.

Here are the steps in building your confidence:

- **Set realistic goals:** Set specific, realistic goals, which match your talents and skills.

31

Obviously a short person would not set a goal of slam-dunking a basketball, but this person might set a goal of becoming an excellent shooter or passer. Identify your own strengths and weaknesses when setting your goals.

- **Having a goal brings about the means:** Once you decide to do something, the means to do it start to show up. When you decide to buy a particular make of car, suddenly you begin to see that car all over the highway and ads for it everywhere. The cars and the ads were there before, but you just didn't notice them. Now you do because you have a goal. When you focus on something, you open your eyes to all the possibilities.
- **Mistakes are stepping-stones:** Instead of viewing mistakes as setbacks, view them as steps toward your goal. When a puppy is learning to climb up and down stairs, it falls down many times but just keeps on adjusting until it does it successfully.
- **Expect success, not failure:** People who are truly confident don't focus on mistakes. They notice their successes. By keeping their focus on reaching the goal, they have the confidence to continue until the goal is achieved. Many people you see as being self-confident weren't born that way; self-confidence takes time and the right attitude.
- **Trust yourself:** If you don't trust yourself, you defeat yourself. You have to learn to go

with your gut instincts. If you see a good pitch to swing at, you can't hold back because you're afraid of striking out.

Learning to Listen to Yourself

You can change the habit of negative thinking to positive thinking. You begin by becoming aware of when you are saying negative things to yourself. Start by keeping track of how many times during the day you say such things. Become aware of the habits that you have.

You may want to keep a note card handy. You can place a check mark on the card each time you put yourself down. When you have done this for a few days you may be surprised at how many marks you have on your card. Once you are aware of the negative things that you say to yourself, you can change them and increase your self-esteem.

Successful people learn to turn their negative thinking around. They reprogram their mental messages to be more helpful. You can do that, too. Once you are aware of the negative things that you say to yourself, you can change them. Whenever you start to say something bad about yourself, STOP. Don't do it.

How Am I Working to Achieve My Goals?

Ask yourself: If I know my goals, what am I doing to achieve them? Is it working?

Sometimes people set goals but never check whether what they are doing is furthering their goals. If what you have been doing is not producing the results you want, ask

Make a list of your goals and keep it on hand wherever you go. That way, you can keep track of your accomplishments and cross off the things you've done!

yourself a very important question: What can I do differently to reach my goals?

Since you create your own behavior, you can change your behavior. You've surely heard the old saying, "If at first you don't succeed, try, try again." Let's change it to, "If at first you don't succeed, do something else." That doesn't mean that you abandon your goal. It means that you abandon the self-defeating behavior that was not moving you toward the goal. If your goal was to get an "A" in your history class, but you got a "C" on your first exam, then you need to find a different way to prepare for your exams.

Commit yourself to create doable, realistic, positive goals, and then move toward them step-by-step. You are choosing a new plan and making a commitment to improve your life.

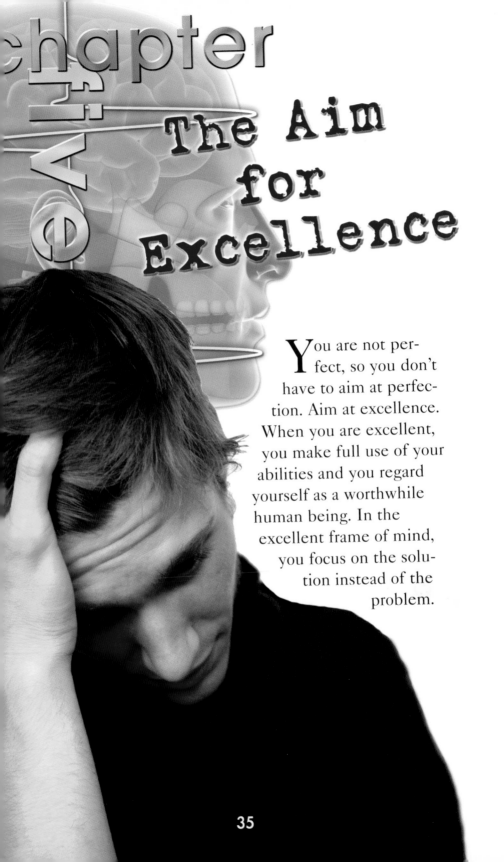

chapter five

The Aim for Excellence

You are not perfect, so you don't have to aim at perfection. Aim at excellence. When you are excellent, you make full use of your abilities and you regard yourself as a worthwhile human being. In the excellent frame of mind, you focus on the solution instead of the problem.

Excellence brings quality into your life by riveting your attention on your goals instead of on any obstacles in the way.

Volunteering, joining a club, or even taking up a new hobby can be ways of getting more control over your life and gaining a sense of accomplishment.

Failure

When you aim for excellence, you realize that you cannot succeed without sometimes failing. Most people view failure as a dead end. But failure is important information in disguise. Failure tells you what not to do. A young person learning to ride a bike fails many times, but every failure brings that young person one step closer to success.

Don't define "failure" as disaster resulting from the inability to succeed. Think of it this way:

- Failure is essential to success.
- You cannot succeed without failing often enough to discover what you need to succeed.
- Failure is the process of gathering information, adjusting your course of action, fine-tuning, and focusing.

Giving up after a few failures is like trying to hit a bull's-eye the first time. It is unrealistic to expect to be on target immediately. You have to fail a number of times to succeed. By failing, you discover ways that don't work. You go step-by-step toward the way that does work. This is how you aim for excellence.

The Power in You

An old fable illustrates how confidence and failure work. A young knight wanted to be a hero by slaying the dragons that menaced his land. One day he found a sword that glowed strangely. He thought it was a magic sword, so he went out and killed a dragon with it. Everyone cheered him. Then the knight killed another dragon and was praised as a mighty warrior. He killed a third dragon, a fourth, a fifth, and so on. But then one day an old man told him that the sword was really a piece of scrap metal that had been thrown away by another knight years ago. That day the young knight went out to kill a dragon, but he never came back.

The power was not in the sword. The power was in him because he had the confidence to face his fears. When he thought the sword had lost its magic, he lost his magic. The only magic involved was the magic he was manufacturing within himself. Self-confidence can only come from inside you. Other people can help you find it though, if you choose to listen to them.

Fame and Self-Esteem

People who become famous for their talent or for their accomplishments are really just like you and me. They were once young with dreams and ambitions of what they wanted to do in life. For many, it was not automatically clear to them or their families that they would ever do anything special with their talents. It took many years of practice, patience, and believing in themselves to

Thomas Edison defied the odds and became one of the most successful inventors of all time. Some of his most famous inventions are the lightbulb and the photograph.

eventually do the things that made them famous. These are human beings just like you. If they can build up their own confidence, so can you.

Thomas Edison

Although he was partly deaf and had only three months of formal schooling, Edison became the greatest inventor of all time, patenting more than one thousand inventions. He experimented thousands of times before he found the secret of the electric light. Even though people laughed at him, he knew that each "failure" was a step toward success. He knew he could create the incandescent bulb, and he did. Edison said, "Genius is 1 percent inspiration and 99 percent perspiration." He realized that he could not just wait for things to happen; he had to make them happen.

Helen Keller

At the age of two, Helen had a serious illness that caused her to become blind, deaf, and unable to speak. Almost everyone thought she would go through life never being able to communicate. But her teacher, Anne Sullivan, never gave up. Eventually Helen learned to read, speak, and write. She became a highly educated woman who wrote many books and helped others who seemed beyond help. Her motto was, "The only way out is through," meaning that you cannot solve problems by running away from them. You have to deal with them head-on. Helen Keller and Anne Sullivan both aimed at excellence and had confidence in themselves and in each other.

Greg Louganis

At different points in his life, Greg was diagnosed as dyslexic (a learning disorder), was put up for adoption, felt unwanted and unloved, kept his homosexuality a secret, and often abused drugs and alcohol. But eventually he turned his life around and became such a skilled diver that he won gold medals in two events at the Olympic Games in 1984 and 1988. At the time, Greg was known as the World's Greatest Diver. An example of his confidence occurred when he scraped his scalp on the edge of a diving board when performing during the 1988 Summer Olympics. Most people would have been too scared to take another dive. But he simply had his scalp stitched and bandaged, got back on the diving board, and made a gold-medal dive. Later, no longer afraid of what people would think of him, he came out as a gay man publicly and stated that he had AIDS. Today, Greg is still alive and well. He speaks regularly to youth clubs, drug and alcohol rehabilitation groups, and organizations for the dyslexic.

Experiencing Fear and Excitement

When you feel fear, you are experiencing a strong emotion that has powerful effects on your body. The same is true when you feel excitement. Most people consider fear and excitement very different experiences. But when you aim for excellence, you know that they are often the same thing.

Situations that used to cause fear can now create excitement. Why? Not because the situations have changed, but because you are doing things and thinking differently.

Finding success in your life means making a lot of sacrifices, learning to come to terms with who you are, and finding confidence in yourself.

Have Patience

Creating self-esteem and confidence is a lifelong, full-time project. It's exciting to discover who you are and what you are capable of doing. Don't think that you are alone in your self-building project. Many people can help you—your family, friends, teachers, and even coworkers.

Have patience with yourself. Even though you are not perfect, you can be excellent. You are a valuable human being who is in the process of becoming everything you are meant to be in this world. You have something special to offer the world that only you can give. It's OK if you don't know what is right this second, but start to take the time to discover your hidden talents. When you focus on your strengths instead of your weaknesses, you will become a happier, more self-confident person.

alienate To cause another person to become unfriendly toward you or to isolate yourself from others.

caution To restrain from an action or decision to avoid harm to yourself.

erroneous Mistaken; containing errors.

impoverished To be deprived of wealth or material possessions.

instinct A gut feeling that tells you what to do.

judgmental Having a tendency to pass off critical opinions of yourself or others.

manufacture The making or producing of something.

perfectionism A personal standard that demands perfection and rejects anything less.

prophecy A prediction of something to come.

sabotage An act or process designed to hurt or hamper.

self-confidence Belief or faith in yourself and your abilities.

self-esteem The pride you have in yourself or your sense of personal worth.

self-fulfilling prophecy Something we expect to happen to ourselves, not because it is our fate, but because we will cause it to happen.

self-reflection A self-examination to find your true feelings or to discover your strengths and weaknesses.

self-talk Thoughts we say to ourselves that influence the way we feel about ourselves or anything else.

visualization Using your mind's eye to practice something without actually doing it.

for more information

Big Brothers Big Sisters of Canada
Les Grands Frères Grandes Soeurs du Canada
3228 South Service Road, Suite 113E
Burlington, ON L7N 3H8
Canada
(905) 639-0461
Website: http://www.bigbrothersbigsisters.ca
Big Brothers Big Sisters of Canada is the leading youth-
    serving organization providing mentoring programs
    across the country.

Big Brothers Big Sisters National Office
230 North 13th Street
Philadelphia, PA 19107
(215) 567-7000
Website: http://www.bbbs.org
Big Brothers Big Sisters provides one-on-one mentors for
    teens across America. The mentors come from all
    walks of life and different backgrounds to help
    young people reach their full potential.

Boys and Girls Clubs of America
1275 Peachtree Street, NE
Atlanta, GA 30309
(404) 487-5700
Website: http://www.bgca.org
The Boys and Girls Clubs of America offer young people
    a safe and supportive place to go for recreational
    activity and personal development.

Canadian Mental Health Association (CMHA)

180 Dundas Street West, Suite 2301
Toronto, ON M5G 1Z8
Canada
(416) 977-5580
Website: http://www.ontario.cmha.ca
CMHA provides courses for parents of children between
the ages of five and thirteen who seek tools to
encourage their children to develop better
self-esteem.

National Association for Self-Esteem (NASE)
P.O. Box 597
Fulton, MD 20759
Website: http://www.self-esteem-nase.org
This organization is committed to building self-esteem. It
offers information on materials such as books and
tapes. NASE also helps connect people who are
interested in self-esteem.

Web Sites

Due to the changing nature of Internet links, Rosen
Publishing has developed an online list of Web sites
related to the subject of this book. This site is updated
regularly. Please use this link to access the list:

http://www.rosenlinks.com/tmh/est

for further reading

Altebrando, Tara. *The Pursuit of Happiness*. New York, NY: MTV, 2006.

Canfield, Jack, and Kent Healy. *The Success Principles for Teens: How to Get from Where You Are to Where You Want to Be*. Deerfield Beach, FL: HCI, 2008.

Cooper, Robert K. *Get Out of Your Own Way: The 5 Keys to Surpassing Everyone's Expectations*. New York, NY: Crown Business, 2006.

Frankl, Viktor. *Man's Search for Meaning*. New York, NY: Pocket Books, 1963.

Harrington, Paul. *The Secret to Teen Power*. New York, NY: Simon & Schuster, 2009.

Maynard, Joyce. *The Cloud Chamber*. New York, NY: SimonSays, 2005.

Palmer, Pat, and Melissa Alberti Froehner. *Teen Esteem: A Self-Direction Manual for Young Adults*. Atascadero, CA: Impact Publishers, 2010.

Pelzer, Dave. *Help Yourself for Teens: Real-Life Advice for Real-Life Challenges*. New York, NY: Plume, 2005.

Schiraldi, Glenn R. *10 Simple Solutions for Building Self-Esteem: How to End Self-Doubt, Gain Confidence & Create a Positive Self-Image*. Oakland, CA: New Harbinger, 2007.

Ursiny, Tim. *The Confidence Plan: How to Build a Stronger You*. Naperville, IL: Sourcebooks, 2005.

Winfree, Woody. *We Are More Than Beautiful: 46 Real Teen Girls Speak Out About Beauty, Happiness, Love and Life*. Naperville, IL: Sourcebooks, 2007.

Zarr, Sara. *Story of a Girl: A Novel*. New York, NY: Little, Brown and Co., 2007.

index

B

Blige, Mary J., 19

C

comfort zone, 9–11
counselor, 10 questions to ask a, 12

D

Depp, Johnny, 7–9
depression screenings, 6

E

Edison, Thomas, 39
external control, 17

F

failure, dealing with, 36
Frankl, Viktor, 23–24

G

goals
    achieving, 33–34
    characteristics of good, 29–30
    managing, 30–33
    and self-talk, 33

I

impoverished thinking, 17–19

K

Keller, Helen, 39

L

Louganis, Greg, 40

M

Man's Search for Meaning, 23–24
mirror, of self-reflection, 6–9

N

negative judgments, 17

O

obesity screenings, 6

P

perfection, and self-talk, 15–16

R

responsibility, 20

S

self-doubt, 26–27
self-esteem, myths and facts
    about, 21
self-talk, 14–15
    negative, 15–20, 26, 33
    positive, 24–25, 27, 33
Sullivan, Anne, 39

T

thought reversal, 26

V

victimization, and self-talk, 19

About the Authors

Betsy S. Morrison is an author and educator. She lives in Dallas, Texas, with her husband and two children.

Ruth Ann Ruiz is the author of nonfiction books for children and teens.

Photo Credits

Cover, p. 1 (top left) © www.istockphoto.com/William Britten; cover, p. 1 (middle left) © www.istockphoto.com/Jaymast; cover, p. 1 (bottom left) © www.istockphoto.com/Anna Minkevich; cover (foreground) © www.istockphoto.com/Justin Horrocks; cover, pp. 1, 3 (head and brain) © www.istockphoto.com/Vasiliy Yakobchuk; p. 3 (laptop) © www.istockphoto.com/Brendon De Suza; pp. 4, 13, 22, 28, 35 (head) © www.istockphoto.com; p. 4 © www.istockphoto.com/Shelly Perry; p. 5 © David Young-Wolff/Alamy; p. 8 Jeff Kravitz/FilmMagic/Getty Images; p. 10 © www.istockphoto.com/Robert Churchill; p. 13 © www.istockphoto.com/Paul Hill; p. 14 © Bob Daemmrich/The Image Works; p. 16 STOCK4B/Getty Images; p. 18 Frazer Harrison/Getty Images; p. 22 © www.istockphoto.com/ericsphotography; pp. 23, 41 Brand X Pictures/Thinkstock; p. 28 © www.istockphoto.com/M. Eric Honeycutt; p. 30 Jupiterimages/Thinkstock; p. 34 iStockphoto/Thinkstock; p. 35 © www.istockphoto.com/Ivar Teunissen; p. 38 Nathan Lazarnick/George Eastman House/Getty Images; interior graphics (books) © www.istockphoto.com/Michal Koziarski.

Editor: Bethany Bryan; Photo Researcher: Amy Feinberg